W9-CWQ-090

The Decoy

The Decoy

Jim Poling Sr.

KEY PORTER BOOKS

The publisher gratefully acknowledges Peter Brown's permission to use photographs of his extraordinary collection of antique decoys in this book.

Copyright © 2001 by Key Porter Books

All rights reserved. No part of this work covered by the copyrights hereon may be reproduced or used in any form or by any means—graphic, electronic or mechanical, including photocopying, recording, taping or information storage and retrieval systems—without the prior written permission of the publisher, or in the case of photocopying or other reprographic copying, a license from the Canadian Copyright Licensing Agency.

National Library of Canada Cataloguing in Publication Data

    Poling, Jim (Jim R.)

ISBN: 1-55263-301-2

1. Decoys (Hunting) 2. Wood-carving. I. Title.

SK335.P64 2001   745.593'6   C2001-900597-0

The publisher gratefully acknowledges the support of the Canada Council for the Arts and the Ontario Arts Council for its publishing program.

We acknowledge the financial support of the Government of Canada through the Book Publishing Industry Development Program (BPIDP) for our publishing activities.

Key Porter Books Limited
70 The Esplanade
Toronto, Ontario
Canada M5E 1R2

www.keyporter.com

Cover design: Peter Maher
Electronic formatting: Jack Steiner Graphic Design

Printed and bound in Spain

01 02 03 04 05 06 6 5 4 3 2 1

When an individual is seen gliding through the woods and close to the observer,

it passes like a thought, and on trying to see it again, the eye searches in vain;

the bird is gone.

JOHN JAMES AUDUBON (1785–1851)

Hooded Merganser (*c.* 1940)

Contents

Introduction

Her eyes are bright and stare knowingly into the empty space ahead, hinting at the history she has witnessed but revealing little. Her paint shows bruises and crazing. Dents along her folded wings and a chip in her perky tail tell of many punt trips through the marsh and untold hours of bobbing and bumping against others of her flock. Gray pencil-point depressions along one side and up her neck are the scars of a shot fired too low in the dim pre-dawn light.

If only she could talk. Would she tell of riding a storm-tossed bay on Lake Erie, or of floating quietly on some Midwest farm pond? Or would she speak of rolling in the tides and tasting the salt water of Chesapeake Bay? Did she live the hard life of daily service in a market gunner's rig, yanked from a wicker basket by hardened hands and tossed roughly into icy waters where she was left for days? Or did she belong to soft-spoken city men who worked her but a few times a year, then dried and caressed her and set her to rest on their clubhouse shelf? How many million ducks have those cold, watchful eyes seen passing through the skies? How many have been coerced by her, calling to her, wheeling and gliding to join her, only to hear the roar and feel the sting of death?

Pondering these mysteries is the joy of decoys. Each one is a piece of history, and discovering that history and situating it within a larger context is a major attraction of studying and collecting. Each decoy tells of a distinct region or individual, while collectively, decoy history reflects the history of North America—of settlement and development, hunting and conservation. Decoys are totems evoking times and cultures long gone, and the growth of the human experience.

The history of the crafted decoy, a genuine North American artifact, is long and rich. Aboriginal peoples used decoys to lure waterfowl well before the birth of Christ. Settlers from Europe, accustomed to trapping ducks with live decoys, adopted the handmade version as they did so many other Native implements, and they applied their woodworking skills to produce bird likenesses in cedar, pine and other soft woods. The evolution of the decoy closely followed the development of North America. As the East flourished and settlement moved west, migratory birds became an important food source. Men began earning a living shooting as many birds as they could to meet the demand of city markets and restaurants. Hundreds of decoys were needed to lure thousands of ducks, geese and others into gun range. When individual carvers could not produce enough, factories began turning out decoys for the market gunning industry.

Inevitably, the birds began to disappear and, with them, the factories and many of the individual carvers. Some craftsmen turned to making waterfowl decoys that were more decorative than working lure, and thus the decoy evolved into an art form. It entered the sphere of folk art and became an important part of the world of antiques and collectibles. Many exceptional and unique waterfowl carvings have come to light in the last few decades, and now the best and the rarest command hundreds of thousands of dollars at auction. Once fashioned in haste, with whatever materials were at hand, to help gather meat, decoys are now viewed as folk art sculpture and often as very worthwhile investments.

They are much more than that, however. Decoys are repositories of important segments of North America's past, reminders of our heritage. They testify to how human excess stresses the natural world. In decoys we see reflected our mistakes: market hunting, destruction of animal habitats, pollution, human encroachment in general, mistakes that have endangered many species of wildlife and destroyed others. On the positive side, decoys can be viewed as symbols of hope, of how we recognize our sins against nature and try to correct them through conservation movements such as Ducks Unlimited, the Audubon Society and many others.

Why has interest in decoys grown so rapidly? Perhaps it's our natural yearning to know and understand our past. Or maybe it's appreciation of the beauty and warmth of things fashioned by hand, especially in a world of molded or stamped synthetics. Decoys reflect the beauty of nature. If only they could talk, what amazing things they would tell us. Then again, if they could talk, there would be less need to collect them.

C H A P T E R   O N E

The Great Flyways

Cork body Canvasback
(*c.* 1865)

I t is a sound like water being released into a dry creek bed, a whispered gurgle gaining strength to become a soft roar before subsiding as if swallowed by some unknown force. It is gone before you comprehend that it was there, and then you question whether it really was. The sound of a thousand wings lifting off a marshy bay and climbing through the morning mist on another flight in the mystery of migration. Dozens of ducks, geese, swans and shorebirds joining others to become dozens of dozens, then hundreds of dozens, along the ancient north-south flyways of North America. The mystery is as old as the human race. Many have studied it; many have written about it. Yet no one fully understands why migratory birds set off on these incredible journeys every spring and autumn. What triggers the urge to move? Where do they draw strength for such huge adventures? What inner navigation system directs them so precisely from summer home to winter home and back again, year after year?

Drake Wood Duck (*c.* 1950)

Calling Duck
(c. 1875)

Biologists, and others schooled in ornithological matters, answer some of the questions and speculate on the rest. Survival is the simplest answer to why birds migrate. Wintering in the Arctic regions is impossible and, conversely, if young were born in the southern areas, they could not survive the heat. But what triggers the migration? Some biologists believe that waterfowl migrate once their bodies tell them they have stored enough fat for the arduous journey. Northern Native hunters will tell you that autumn ducks have more leg-bone marrow and shoulder fat than spring ducks. It is known that some songbirds increase their body weight by up to 40 percent before spring and autumn

2

migrations. The ruby-throated hummingbird gains .07 ounces (2 g) of fat for the incredible journey from North America to its winter quarters in Mexico.

Over the decades, some answers have gained prominence only to be later proven wrong through the advancement of human knowledge. For instance, followers of the Greek philosopher Aristotle believed that when birds disappeared in late autumn, they hibernated in caves, marshes and hollow trees. Aristotle also advanced the theory that because one species sometimes arrived as another was leaving, the two species were actually one, changing plumage through transmutation. Other societies believed that birds went to the moon for the winter and flew back in the spring. Some people, unable to comprehend how smaller birds can fly thousands of miles, continue to believe that they hitch rides on the backs of larger birds.

The Native people living along the great flyways of North America before the coming of the Europeans saw waterfowl and other migrating birds in biblical proportions. Horizon-filling clouds of birds traveling from northern Canada and Alaska to southern destinations converged in four major flyways: the Atlantic coastal area, the Mississippi Valley, the Central Great Plains and the Pacific Coast. The earliest explorers and settlers of the continent reported a darkening of the skies as flocks of thousands blocked the sun. The surfaces of ponds and lakes on the Great Plains were black with birds in spring and fall, as were the shallower shores of the southern Great Lakes and the bays and estuaries along the northwest Atlantic coast.

Samuel de Champlain, founder of New France and explorer of much of New England, described birds on islands off the coasts of what are now Nova Scotia and Maine in the early 1600s: ". . . the abundance of birds is so great that no one would believe it possible unless he had seen it. . . ." Thomas Morton, a chronicler of seventeenth-century American life, wrote of seeing a thousand geese before the mouth of his gun. And John J. Audubon, ornithologist and painter, recorded after viewing thousands of migrating passenger pigeons: ". . . they take to wing, producing by the flapping of their wing a noise like the roar of distant thunder. . . ."

Even after many decades of settlement and uncontrolled hunting had decimated migratory bird populations, their numbers still amazed travelers. Warburton Pike, an Englishman who explored the Arctic to see muskoxen and learn about Native life, wrote with awe about wildfowl viewed in the early 1890s:

Scientists in the U.S. and Canada band more than 500,000 migratory birds a year as a means of collecting information for developing conservation policies.

The Arctic Tern holds the record for long distance bird migration. It travels 10,000 miles (16,000 km) from the North Pole to the South Pole and back again every year.

White and Grey wavies and ducks of many kinds were flying overhead in large flocks, and rising in front of the canoe at every bend of the stream; plovers and other wading birds were screaming over the marshes . . . Without going out of our way to hunt, we could have loaded the canoe with wildfowl, but of course only killed as many as we required for food.

For the Native peoples, the coming and going of the birds signaled changes of season and of living style. The first birds moving south generated an urgency to prepare for the hungry, cold and snowy months ahead. A flock of spring ducks brought the promise of easier living. The returning birds were more than a signal of changing seasons, however; they were food, a much-appreciated change from the birds, fish and mammals that had been frozen or dried for winter consumption. They were also elusive, their ability to fly something that humans watched with envy and dreamed of emulating. Hunting them was difficult and required great patience and stealth. It always involved going to where the birds were already gathered, and creeping up on them while they fed in clearings or on the water.

Some tribes copied foxes, who found that by prancing in silly fashion at water's edge they could attract ducks whose curiosity overwhelmed their sense of caution. The Indians hid in reeds and wiggled fox skins on shore to lure their quarry within arrow or netting range. The Europeans practiced a similar type of hunting in the old countries, training Toller dogs to attract waterfowl. The Toller breed was later introduced in North America, when early sportsmen in southwestern Nova Scotia bred foxlike dogs and trained them to entice waterfowl and then retrieve them after they were shot. The curiosity of ducks was often so strong that they would swim to within a few feet of shore, or even walk onto land and stare at the antics.

Somewhere back in the mists of time, a Native hunter, perhaps one of the Inuit of Alaska or a woodlands Indian, developed the concept of decoying with objects that looked like birds. This innovation changed hunting substantially. One might think, when the weapons were bow and arrow, spears, nets and even hand-thrown stones, what difference would it make if the hunter went to the ducks or the ducks came to him? After the first arrow flew, the ducks would be gone. Decoying, however, improved hunting significantly. Formerly, a flock was approached and, once disturbed, it was gone. The

Decoy carving was confined almost exclusively to North America until relatively recently. Now carving and collecting have started to gain popularity throughout the world. For example, the British Decoy Wildfowl Carvers Association, which was formed in 1990 to generate interest in wildfowl carving, accepts members from around the globe.

Bufflehead drake
(c. 1880s)

development of decoys allowed the hunter to hide in one spot, luring flocks to land in front of him, shooting or netting as the birds were most vulnerable, at that awkward moment of landing. Certainly that startled flock was gone with the first arrow shot, but the skies were filled with others who were unaware of what was going on below, especially in the dusky light of early morning or evening.

Captain F. W. Beecher of the British navy described Native people of the Northwest decoying waterfowl into a net during his 1825 voyage to the Bering Strait:

Hollow Blue Bill drake
(c. 1890)

They construct large nets with bulrushes and repair to such river as are the resort of their game, where they fix a long pole upright on each bank, with one end of the net attached to the pole on the opposite side of the river to themselves. Several artificial ducks made of rushes are then set afloat upon the water between the poles as a decoy; and the Indians, who have a line fastened to one end of the net, and passed through a hole in the upper end of the pole that is near them, wait the arrival of their game in concealment. When the birds approach, they suddenly extend the net across the river by pulling upon the line, and interrupt them in their flight, when they fall stunned into a large purse in the net and are captured.

Obviously, no one knows when the first decoy was used, but certainly it was before the time of Christ, and likely long before. Archaeologists working in Lovelock Cave, 80 miles (140 km) northeast of Reno, Nevada, in 1924 unearthed a basket of 11 remarkable canvasback duck decoys made of reeds by ancient Indians. Three of the decoys were works in progress, but eight were realistically painted, and some had feathers attached to their sides to make them more lifelike. These precious artifacts are housed at the Smithsonian Institution's National Museum of the American Indian in New York. Radiocarbon dating has given them an average age of 2,160 years, making them the world's oldest known duck decoys.

Baron Louis-Armand Lahontan, the French adventurer and soldier who explored New France and New England, hunted waterfowl with Indians in the area of Lake Champlain. He described the experience in a letter in 1687, later published in his *New Voyages to North America*:

> The first spot we took up was upon the side of a marsh or fen, of four or five leagues in circumference: and after we had fitted up our Hutts, the savages made Hutts upon water in several places. These Hutts were made of branches and leaves of Trees and contain three or four men. For a Decoy they have the skins of Geese and Ducks, dry'd and stuff'd with Hay. The two feet being made fast with two nails to a small light plank, which

Root head decoys were used to attract wildfowl into shooting range. Makers carved the natural bend in the root of a small tree to shape a head. Basically just heads and necks, the root decoys were pushed into the ground to make them look like birds standing in the grass along a shoreline.

Above left: Hollow Canvasback drake (*c.* 1900)
Left: Canvasback drake (*c.* pre-1900)

Hollow Redhead hen
(*c.* 1880)

floats around the Hutt. The place being frequented by wonderfull numbers of geese, ducks, bustards, teals and an infinity of other waterfowls . . . when these Fouls see the stuff'd Skins swimming with the Heads erected, as if they were alive, they repair to the same place, and so give the savages an opportunity of shooting them either flying upon the water, after which the savages get into their Canows and gather them up.

Use of handmade wildfowl decoys was almost exclusively a North American practice. European and other societies used live birds for decoying, but there is little evidence that handmade decoys were popular to any extent beyond the New World. The word "decoy" even had different meanings on the two sides of the ocean: in North America a decoy was a handmade bird replica, while in England it was a setup or place where birds were trapped. The word comes from the Dutch *ende-kooi*, meaning "cage" or "trap," and it is rooted in the European practice of placing live birds in a cage to attract others from the wild. The English adopted the practice from the Dutch, using boats and dogs to drive ducks into decoys, some of which were elaborate cage traps with long funneled entrances. There are ancient records of three thousand ducks being taken at one time at Spalding, Lincolnshire, and four thousand at Deeping Fen. Live decoys were frequently used to lure pigeons. Hunters captured passenger pigeons, sewed the live birds' eyes shut and tied their legs to a perch, or stool. When the hunter spotted an approaching flock, he pulled the string to make the stool wobble and cause the blind bird to lose balance and flap its wings. Flying pigeons saw the flapping and assumed that the bird on the stool had found a new source of food. Hence the origin of the term "stool pigeon." In fact, the word "stool" is still used in some regions of North America to mean "decoy."

Many Native decoys were much less elaborate, less realistic than the Lovelock find. They were shaped mounds of mud, or rocks stacked to resemble a bird—anything that could form a silhouette when seen from above, at a distance. Even today, waterfowl hunters will use simple silhouettes in areas where shooting competition is not heavy and where ducks or geese can be more easily lured. But the Native peoples, keen observers of

wildlife, knew that success in attracting waterfowl lay in convincing flying birds that the flock below was the real thing, and decoys that looked like real ducks had the best chance of doing so.

The First Peoples created decoys with whatever natural materials were available, and there was no shortage of ingenuity. Tule, other types of bulrush, or grasses were bound into bird-like shapes. The Cree of James Bay in northern Canada wound spruce twigs into the shape of geese. Others used sticks and grasses covered with feathers, or stuffed duck and geese skins with grass. Cree spruce-twig decoys had hollow heads through which snow or water reflected, giving the appearance of light striking the white throat of a Canada goose. Another Native group curled strips of white birchbark around the necks of their decoys for the same purpose.

Europeans trying to survive in the vast North American wilderness seized on the decoy just as they did the canoe, the toboggan, the snowshoe and Native medicines. The decoy quickly became an important hunting tool, advanced by the human urge to be creative and later by the need for more verisimilitude in areas of strong hunting pressure. With their rich woodworking heritage the Europeans advanced the craft of decoying by carving their birds from blocks of wood, thus enabling multi-year use.

Decoy use at the start of the nineteenth century was mainly by individuals hunting food for their dinner table. The first written account of the use of duck decoys is believed to be that in Alexander Wilson's *American Ornithology*, the celebrated nine-volume work published between 1808 and 1814. It notes:

> In some ponds frequented by these birds, five or six wooden figures, cut and painted as
> so to represent ducks, and sunk, by pieces of lead nailed to their bottoms, so as to float
> at the usual depth on the surface, are anchored in a favorable position for being raked
> from concealment of brush, etc., on the shore. The appearance of these usually attracts
> passing flocks, which alight and are shot down. Sometimes eight or ten of these painted
> wooden ducks are fixed on a wooden frame in various swimming postures, and secured

The importance of decoy size in attracting ducks has been hotly debated since the early days of waterfowl hunting. Do larger decoys really attract more ducks? The conventional wisdom today is that, yes, magnum decoys are more easily seen and do pull in more ducks in areas where hunting is heavy. On the other hand, smaller and lighter decoys work just as well in areas where ducks are plentiful and hunters are few.

Common Merganser hen (year unknown)

Pintail (*c.* 1870)

to the bow of the gunner's skiff, projecting before it in such a manner that the weight of the frame sinks the figures to their proper depth.

Two basic types of wood decoy—floaters and stickups—were the mainstays of early North American waterfowling. Floaters were the carved blocks set out in ponds and at the edges of lakes and oceans. Stickups were often simply carved wildfowl heads or body silhouettes on sticks that were pushed into the ground along a shoreline to give the appearance of birds resting and feeding. Stickups with body forms were designed for fields. Some inventive craftsmen even created flying decoys that moved across pieces of wire.

Decoying is based on migratory birds' passion for flocking. Ducks are gregarious, and when they want to feed and rest, they will join others already on the water or the land,

Canvas-covered
Canvasback (*c.* 1880)

banking into the wind and landing in open spaces among the others, where they tuk and quack to each other in a sociable setting. Successful decoying involves laying out convincing patterns that allow favorable landing within shotgun range. Patterns vary because of geography, wind conditions and the characteristics of the birds.

Each decoy was set out with a line attached to a weight that kept the decoy anchored. Weights were usually lead, sometimes salvaged from the welds of metal tea boxes. Their size, shape and weight depended on the type of water and the bottom below it. The preferences and quirks of the maker, and the type of raw material available, also influenced style. Lead was inserted into decoy bottoms as ballast to provide realistic floating characteristics.

The first artificial duck calls are believed to have been developed along the Mississippi Flyway circa 1850.

Hunting decoys were carved for good visibility, not detail. They were usually larger than a real bird, with thinner heads and exaggerated backs to provide a better profile. How they "drew" was far more important than how they looked. The use of bird calls became an important supplement for attracting certain species of ducks and geese to the decoys.

White pine and cedar were the most popular woods for decoys, along with white juniper, tupelo, cottonwood and cypress. Cedar bodies with white pine heads were common because the cedar resisted rot and pine was easiest to shape. The process of carving and the tools employed were basic. The carver cut a block of wood the length of the body required. Rough shaping was done with a hatchet, then with somewhat finer strokes from a drawknife. A rasp handled the finishing. Heads were almost always carved separately and were removable from the body. This made transporting easier, eliminated the problem of breaking narrow necks and allowed for heads to be set in different, more realistic, positions. The earliest wooden decoys were quickly and crudely carved by today's standards, not because the carvers lacked talent but because nothing elaborate was required. In those days, anything that gave the appearance of a duck in poor light was enough to pull in flocks of birds. Later, the ducks would grow skittish after exposure to fusillades from hunters stationed at every corner of a marsh.

The waterfowl hunter of the early nineteenth century was usually a man with a few blocks and a flintlock gathering what ducks and geese he could for the larder. The flintlock was awkward and slow. Before firing, powder and shot had to be stuffed into the barrel and the powder pan filled, and this process was repeated for each shot. Great patience and dexterity were needed to gather ducks in large numbers, but some hunters did. There is a record of one man who, in 1872, shot 1,365 ducks in 17 days, an average of 80 per day, with a single-barreled muzzleloader. The firearm was obviously his preference, because cartridge guns had replaced flintlocks by then.

The simple life of shooting for home consumption changed during the course of the nineteenth century, as landmark developments in North American life converged to create a new age of mechanization. Exploration of the American West following the

Swan (c. 1880)

Hollow Canada Goose
(*c.* 1865)

Louisiana Purchase in 1803 opened vast territories for settlement. The steam engine was invented and put to use on the railroads, carrying immigrants to settlements that soon swelled into towns and cities. The U.S. population grew from 7.2 million in 1810 to 12.8 million in 1830. This burgeoning population, now stretching from the east coast to the west, needed food. The forests, plains and marshes were filled with game, and all that was required was someone to shoot it in large numbers and transport it quickly. At roughly the same time, firearms development leaped forward into the age of cartridges and repeating arms. These guns, together with the new rail lines, allowed for harvest-style

Hollow Canada Goose
(*c.* 1875)

Female Mallard (year unknown)

The passenger pigeon received its name from the fact that it traveled rapidly from place to place in search of food. Early in the history of North America people referred to them as "pigeons of passage," and their Latin name, *Ectopisles migratorius*, means migratory wanderers.

waterfowl kills that could be shipped greater distances without spoiling. Wide-scale commercial hunting demanded more decoys, and individual carvers were unable to supply the demand; so factories opened, bringing decoy making into the industrial age.

Market hunting, the wholesale killing of wildlife as a business, confirmed the decoy as an important part of American life and helped in its later elevation to the status of artwork. However, it also marked a regrettable era in which natural resources were depleted, in some cases to unrecoverable levels, by human greed. When market hunting ended after the turn of the twentieth century, it had taken with it the rushing roar of hundreds of thousands of beating wings. It was no longer possible to walk out onto the plains and see herds of buffalo. And no one ever again would hear the distinctive kee-kee-kee of that most plentiful of all migratory birds, the passenger pigeon.

Black-breasted Plover (c. pre-1900)

CHAPTER TWO

Market Hunters, Market Carvers

Canvas-covered
Canvasback (*c.* 1880)

North America in the early nineteenth century was young, hard-working and always hungry. Farming was primitive from today's perspective, but natural food was abundant in the forests and fields and along the waterways. Hunting and fishing were critical to the food supply. Individuals continued to shoot game for their families, but as the population grew and spilled west of the Great Lakes and Appalachians, markets demanded more intensive hunting. With market hunting, the harvest of wildlife was no longer based on personal need. The object was to kill as much as possible every day in order to fill the barrels that would ride wagons and rail cars into markets at Chicago, Toronto, New York, Boston, St. Louis, San Francisco and other towns whose population bursts were creating the continent's first cities.

Lowhead Blue Bill (*c.* 1900)

Market hunting of a sort has always been part of North American life. Native hunters and trappers and a variety of woodsmen killed game for sale to the settlements. In the nineteenth century, however, market hunting became part of a distinct economic system involving harvesting, transportation, finance, wholesaling, and mercantile and food distribution operations.

San Francisco is an example of how explosive growth created a prosperous market-hunting industry. At the beginning of 1848 its population comprised 800 lonely souls. Five years later, the gold rush of 1849 had pushed that to 50,000, with tens of thousands

more passing through each year from the mines. By that time more than 250,000 gold seekers had trudged into California, all seeking a place to sleep and food to eat. Boarding houses and small restaurants were thrown up, and gathering food for these masses became a profitable business. Waterfowl were slaughtered in huge numbers throughout the San Francisco Bay area and on Oakland's Lake Merritt. Lower Klamath Lake in northern California and southern Oregon became a major waterfowl slaughter center for the urban food markets. The toll on birds there became so extensive that William Dutcher, president of the Audubon Society, reported in the early 1900s that market

Hollow Pintail drake
(*c.* 1910)

hunters shipped 120 tons of waterfowl from the region in a single year.

Some of the earliest successes in market hunting took place about 1840 on Long Island, which teemed with migratory birds that were shot by the hundreds one evening and graced the tables of New York restaurants the next. Areas of the Great Lakes, particularly lakes Erie and St. Clair, and the St. Lawrence River were extensively market hunted to satisfy the markets in Detroit, Chicago and New York.

Wisconsin ornithologists Kumlien and Holister described hunting for the Chicago market in their 1903 book *Birds of Wisconsin*: "For years the dowitchers [sandpiper species] were shot over decoys on Lake Koshonong for the Chicago market, in May and the first half of June, until they have been practically exterminated. We are informed that from 1887 to 1890 two men averaged 10 dozen a day during May and June!" At that rate the two hunters would have bagged more than 5,000 birds during each year's hunting season. One market hunter who worked the Texas gulf coast calculated that he had shot 360,000 ducks over 16 years. The Wisconsin ornithologists also reported: "So common are the red-backs (sandpipers) at times that we saw, in May 1899, fifty-three individuals killed by the discharge of a double-barreled shot gun...."

Hollow Ringneck hen (year unknown)

28

Cork body
Canvasback (*c.* 1865)

There were clear differences between market and recreational hunting. The market hunter fired into a flock of ducks hoping to kill or wound as many as possible. He also shot ducks on the water, whence comes the phrase *a sitting duck*. For the sports hunter, on the other hand, shooting individual ducks on the wing was a test of skill.

Market hunters in Kansas packed their birds in 55-gallon drums, covering each layer with wax as a preservative. Others used canvas bags, bushel baskets and wooden cartons, depending on the shipping distance. In Nebraska, hunters would fill a wagon with

Eskimo curlews and plovers, then take them to be cleaned while they went out and shot more. Two Boston game dealers in 1890 reported receiving eight barrels of Eskimo curlews and 12 barrels of golden plovers from the Midwest; the curlews were packed 300 to a barrel, the plovers 720 to a barrel. Streams of packed birds flowed into New York's Fulton Market, where canvasbacks sold for $1 a pair in 1873, mallards for 75 cents a pair and quail for $1.50 a dozen.

Only weather and the physical limitations of handling so many birds acted as checks on the market hunters' killing. Harry M. Walsh wrote in his 1971 book *The Outlaw Gunner* that one market hunter shot the marshes of Elliott Island, Maryland, for 18 years ending in 1918, killing an average of 10,000 birds a year. "The limiting factor in his daily kill of two hundred birds was, simply, carrying them off the marsh."

Faster and bigger guns made it possible to take more birds in less time. Battery guns— multiple-barreled shotguns—and large-gauge shotguns that were effective over great distances were designed to quicken the killing process. The deadliest of all were the Big Guns or Night Guns, English punt guns adapted for North American use. Basically small cannons, they were packed with a quarter to half a pound ($^1/_8$ kg to $^1/_4$ kg) of black powder and stuffed with up to two pounds (1 kg) of shot, and they could kill dozens of ducks with one blast. They were 8 feet to 12 feet long (2.4 m to 3.6 m), weighed more than 100 pounds (45 kg), and had bores of $^1/_4$ inches to 2 inches (0.65 cm to 5 cm). They were mounted in shallow-draft duck punts in which the hunter would lay prone. Sometimes the discharge of the gun was so great that it sent the boat sailing backwards.

Punt gunning was quickly outlawed, but it continued to be widespread at night. A punt gunner would quietly paddle towards a raft of diving ducks, such as canvasbacks and, once within firing range, kill 75 to 100 with a single shot. The water glistened with gold where bags of corn were dumped as bait. Often a lantern was shone to blind the ducks and make them swim into the light. Such jacklighting of birds and animals was a common practice in North America. The Native peoples hunted waterfowl and deer at night, mesmerizing them with the light from flaming torches. The American frontier painter George Caitlin captured one such night hunt in his 1846 painting *Deer Hunting by Torchlight in Bark Canoes*. Jacklighting is still performed by poachers, but it is against the law in most jurisdictions.

One of the many legendary stories in North American gunning concerns a double

Decoy carvers tended to produce more drakes than hens — sometimes the ratio was 80 to 20 — because male plumage is brighter and was thought to be more visible to flying ducks.

Hollow Lowhead
Whistlers (*c.* 1900)

Overleaf: Whistler
hen (*c.* 1920)

Hollow Black Duck
(year unknown)

gunning battery set up off Bellport, Long Island, in December 1898. Crews of men spelled each other off as shooting began at daybreak and continued until sundown. The count for the day was 640 ducks, sold at 25 cents apiece.

From Flintlock to Breech-loader

Firearms technology advanced quickly in the nineteenth century. The flintlock ruled as the king of personal weapons beginning in the 1600s, but about 1825 the percussion cap system, in which a gun hammer struck a cap and set off a tiny explosion in the firing chamber, replaced the flint and powder pan mechanism. Its life was cut short, however, when cartridge guns appeared after the Dreyse needle gun was designed and manufactured in 1837. Double breech-loading shotguns appeared around 1855, and the Civil War a few years later brought more developments. By 1871 the hammerless breech-loader appeared, about the same time as choke boring, which made for more effective shot patterns.

Hunters who, 50 years earlier, had rammed powder, ball and paper down a barrel and then primed the gun with powder now simply cracked open a double-barreled gun, quickly inserted two cartridges, snapped it shut and fired. Boring of chokes allowed more effective shot-killing patterns for different birds in varying hunting circumstances. By 1900, John R. Browning had developed the semi-automatic shotgun, allowing hunters to fire shot after shot simply by squeezing the trigger.

Decoys, which up to that time were often nothing more than wooden blocks quickly and roughly whittled into shape, advanced at the same time. Carving decoys had been a hobby, but the explosion of hunting for market, plus the growth of recreational hunting, made production carving not only possible but necessary. By the mid-nineteenth century, carving had become a cottage industry, and one- and two-man operations were soon followed by decoy factories. A carving operation even existed at a Canadian federal penitentiary. Inmates began turning out decoys for sale in the mid-nineteenth century, and the practice continued on and off for almost a century.

Market hunters used huge rigs of 200 to 300 decoys, and with hunting becoming an industry it was profitable for carvers to make decoys full-time. Styles became a bit more realistic, and experimentation even produced the first rubber decoys (1867) and some metal versions, but wood was the standard. Some hunters used live duck decoys, and although nothing could match them for luring ability, they had to be fed, tended and trained, and transportation and positioning were awkward. In 1909 a pair of live mallards sold for $3.50, which was no small price. They were so effective that they were banned from waterfowl hunting in 1935.

For gunners, whittling during the winter months was a comfort after the harsh life of hunting the marshes. Market gunning was not a romantic occupation, and the pay was disappointing for the amount of labor involved. Work began before sun-up and finished long after sundown. The marshes were wet and cold, and getting to them in rough weather in open boats was dangerous. Dozens of decoys had to be set in the water, and later removed by hands stiffened and cracked by constant exposure to wind and water. The sheer volume of killing meant much vigorous manual labor. Wet ducks were gathered into bags or baskets and hauled away. Hunters who couldn't afford to hire help

There were so many passenger pigeons in the early 1700s that people in the young towns of North America stood on their roofs and knocked them from the sky with broomsticks.

Some towns, such as Quebec City and Philadelphia, passed laws prohibiting shooting of passenger pigeons in the streets because this had become a public safety hazard.

plucked and gutted the birds themselves. Equipment had to be maintained, lead weights for decoy anchors poured, shot shells reloaded. Many a gunner must have gone deaf from the constant pounding of 12-gauge, or even 10- and 8-gauge, double-barreled shotguns. Shooting could be so frantic that most hunters carried two or three guns, alternating them so that they would not overheat and damage the barrels. It was not uncommon for a market gunner to wear out one gun a year.

Frank Forester's *Manual for Young Sportsmen* (1871) described marsh hunting: "It is hard, earnest downright work. It requires a man, who not only can rough it, but who loves to rough it, for it's [sic] own sake—who can endure cold, wet, fatigue...."

The market hunting industry was so effective that its toll on the bird population attracted comment. Expressions of concern were not acted upon until late in the century, however. Tens of thousands of barrels, bags and cartons of wildfowl regularly streamed from the countryside to city markets for much of the nineteenth century and into the twentieth. One market hunter wrote of hunting on February 5, 1906, with his partner in southern California. They shot 218 geese in one hour, and their count for the day was 450, all of which had to be cleaned and shipped in a panic because the weather had turned warm.

Market hunting wiped out huge populations of plovers and Eskimo curlews. The latter species is now believed to be extinct, and plovers are estimated to number only 100,000 to 200,000 worldwide. Market hunters turned to curlews and plovers after the passenger pigeon population thinned in the latter part of the nineteenth century. These were slim birds with blue-gray plumage and red breasts, and their meat was much sought after in North America and Europe. It is estimated that North American populations numbered three to five billion before serious hunting began.

In 1818, John James Audubon wrote about viewing passenger pigeons outside his Henderson, Kentucky, home:

The air was literally filled with pigeons. The light of noon day was obscured as by an

eclipse; let us make a column of one mile in breadth, which is far below the average size,

Blue Bill (c. 1900)

and suppose it passes over us without interruption for three hours, at a rate of one mile in the minute. This will give us a parallelogram of 180 miles by 1, covering 180 square miles. Allowing 2 pigeons to the square yard, we have 115,136,000 pigeons in one flock.

Serious market hunting of the pigeons began about 1850, and professional pigeoners, capturing their quarry in nets, made $10 to $40 a day. Sometimes a single net would catch ten dozen birds, and there was one report of 25,000 pigeons being taken in one outing in Michigan. Passenger pigeons were also used for shotgun practice in the sport of trap shooting. These birds could fly up to 90 miles (144 km) an hour and offered a great test of shooting skill. Shooting clubs would run through hundreds of dozens of the birds at each shooting meet. Even small songbirds were netted and placed in trap boxes for release at trap shooting meets. Shorebirds were decoyed and shot during the summer as a gunning tune-up for the fall water-fowl season.

Throughout most of the nineteenth century, it was inconceivable that passenger pigeons,

One of the last great roosts of passenger pigeons was at Prairie du Chien, Wisconsin, in 1871. A memorial stone there commemorates that event.

Hooded Mergansers (*c.* 1900)

41

Hollow Hooded
Mergansers (*c.* 1900)

which blackened skies and shattered tree branches by the sheer weight of their incredible numbers, could ever disappear. Yet, a mere one hundred years after Audubon's sighting of millions of the birds, the last passenger pigeon, named Martha, died on September 1, 1914, in a Cincinnati zoo. She is now on display at the Smithsonian in Washington, D.C.

The Toll for the Millinery Trade

Migratory birds not only made for millions of meals in American homes and restaurants; they also played a major role in the millinery and bedding industries. Ducks and geese, eider ducks in particular, were hunted for their downy feathers, which were used to stuff pillows and mattresses. The most colorful ducks, shorebirds and plume birds, such as terns and herons, were shot so their feathers could decorate the fancy hats and dresses of the times. Three feather sales in London, England, in 1911 provide a glimpse of the numbers of birds used in the feather trade. William Hornaday, director of the New York Zoological Park, gathered information from those sales and calculated that the number of feathers sold represented the corpses of 223,490 birds. The millinery trade in the 1880s wiped out puffin populations on some islands along the coast of Maine. The century-long commercial slaughter of birds for food and fashion seems almost incomprehensible today. We ask ourselves: What was going on in the heads of these people? Did they

At the end of the pigeon era in 1914, one game dealer lamented: *"They went as a cannon ball is dropped into the ocean, now in plain sight, then a splash, a circle of ripples and nothing."*

Hollow Canvasback
drake (*c. 1920*)

really believe there could be no end to this natural resource? Some probably did. Others simply did not think about it. Market hunters were no different from people today who go to work in industries that impact negatively on the global environment. A worker in a coal-generated electricity plant probably knows that the gases expelled are detrimental to wildlife and human life, but this person needs to work and trusts that ongoing improvements and legislative action provide a balance between pollution and the need for jobs. The market hunters were simply doing work that was provided by the economic system of the day.

While the handmade decoy was exclusively a North American bird-hunting tool, Americans were not alone in the great migratory bird depletion of the nineteenth and early twentieth centuries. Millions of birds were consumed through duck trapping and shooting in Europe. One small example of the numbers involved and the attitude of the times is provided by Englishman W. Halliday in his 1917 *Book of Migratory Birds*, in which he describes shooting at Holy Island off the northeastern coast of England:

> In such favorable weather, and with plenty of frost, a bag from 60 to 80 geese may be obtained during the month of January. I have obtained as many as 200 after Christmas, but with every exertion, as well as with good luck, the average number would seldom exceed 80 of these excessively wary fowl, and in mild winters perhaps not more than from 40 to 50.

These were times of wildlife abundance, and the people's attitude was that wildlife were provided for their use. Fortunately, the results of such excess became increasingly evident and alarm was sounded in two unexpected quarters: the well-off of the cities raised concerns about the effects of the millinery trade, while sportsmen spoke out about the loss of wildlife for their recreational pursuits. Sports hunters who belonged to clubs where kills were recorded in a register were among the first to have hard evidence of waterfowl decline. The following chart from the Winous Point Club near Port Clinton, Ohio, and published in *Our Feathered Game* in 1903 tells the story in stark figures:

Year	Canvasbacks	Mallards	Blue-winged Teal
1880	665	1,319	2,110
1885	237	943	1,019
1890	697	394	603
1895	72	218	21
1900	1	232	–

William Hornaday made a powerful statement about uncontrolled wildlife hunting in his 1913 book *Our Vanishing Wild Life: Its Extermination and Preservation*. Regretfully, his book is shockingly racist, with attacks on blacks, poor whites and people of

Bird banding grew out of the panic over the dramatic decline of migratory birds. The U.S. Bureau of Biological Survey was established in 1920 and given responsibility for bird banding programs. In 1923, Canada formed the Canadian Bird Banding Office.

Hollow Pintails
(c. 1920)

non-American background, but it gives a clear picture of the extent of the bird slaughter. Hornaday wrote:

> Of all the meat-shooters, the market-gunners who prey on wild fowl and ground game birds for the big city markets are the most deadly to wild life. Enough geese, ducks, brant, quail, ruffed grouse, prairie chickens, heath hens and wild pigeons have been butchered by gunners and netters for "the market" to have stocked the whole world.

Hornaday gathered statistics from the Louisiana Game Commission to show that in the 1909–10 hunting season (a full year) more than 3.5 million waterfowl were killed. The total number of all birds reported killed during that season, including shorebirds and upland game, was 5.7 million.

In 1886, George Bird Grinnell, editor of *Forest and Stream*, spoke out about the slaughter of the birds and promoted the formation of a society named in honor of John

Cork body
Canvasback
(*c.* 1920)

J. Audubon. The fledgling organization gathered 38,000 members in just three months, but it fell apart in 1888 because it didn't have the administrative structure to meet the demand. Women upset by the killing of birds for their feathers formed the Massachusetts Audubon Society in 1896. Audubon Societies followed in other states.

The Audubon movement received a national voice in 1899 when Frank Chapman, an ornithologist with the American Museum of Natural History in New York, started *Bird Lore* magazine. Chapman wanted people to count birds, not shoot them, and his work started the annual bird census that continues to this day, in which thousands of birders participate. Audubon's William Dutcher hired wardens in 1900 to patrol important bird nesting sites. Three of these wardens were killed by poachers.

These movements against large-scale hunting, and market hunting in particular, received a boost when avid hunter and conservationist Theodore Roosevelt became president eight days after the assassination of William McKinley on September 6, 1901. The new century saw public outrage over market hunting usher in a storm of legislative action. Roosevelt promoted wildlife refuges and was vice-president when the Lacey Act of 1900 was passed by Congress to stop the killing of birds for plumes. This was followed by Roosevelt's executive order of 1903 declaring Pelican Island in Florida the first federal bird sanctuary. Audubon members fought for passage of the 1910 New York State Audubon Plumage Law that banned the sale of native bird plumes in the state.

The writing was on the wall for market hunting when, in 1913, the Weeks–McLean Act was passed, establishing federal control over migratory birds and ending the spring hunting that had been devastating to breeding birds. The act also allowed the setting of hunting seasons. Three years later came the most powerful document ever produced for migratory bird protection: the Migratory Bird Treaty between the U.S. and Great Britain, which was acting for Canada (then basically still a British colony). The treaty became law when passed by Congress in 1918. It was amended in 1937 to include Mexico and to provide for formal co-operation to protect migratory birds throughout the continent.

Market hunting may have been legally abolished, but it was not eliminated. The trade in waterfowl was an industry and nothing could stop it dead in its tracks. Market gunning went underground, ebbing and flowing in direct relationship to the amount of law enforcement directed at it. Market gunners and game officers throughout the U.S. and Canada literally waged war over waterfowl, each side slinking through the night

All U.S. federal agencies are now required to follow protocols before taking any actions or setting any policies that might have a negative impact on waterfowl populations. The protocols were ordered in January 1999 in an Executive Order signed by former President Clinton.

marshes trying to outwit the other. The Dirty Thirties saw an upsurge of illegal hunting when families turned to poaching to feed themselves, but gunning for profit continued through the forties and even into the fifties and sixties. In 1954, federal undercover agents purchased 1,300 illegal ducks from one market gunning operation in California. A U.S. Fish and Wildlife Service undercover agent testified before Congress in the 1960s that illegal market gunning continued to take 500,000 birds a year.

Market gunning is now almost non-existent, because the market for ducks is greatly diminished. The urban societies of North America are more likely to favor a domestically fattened mallard served in a fine restaurant than a wild one shot in a marsh. Individual overshooting or shooting out of season continues, but it is certainly not on the market

Hollow Whistler drake (year unknown)

hunting scale. The real money for modern poachers lies in shooting for the black market trade in animal parts for medicines.

Loss of wetlands, critical breeding grounds for many migratory birds, has proven to be much more of an issue in waterfowl survival than controlled hunting. In fact, some people, hunters and non-hunters alike, point to habitat loss, pollution, interference with migration and human encroachment in general when making the argument that today's society should not be too harsh in its judgment of the market gunners and the people who carved their deadly decoys. Market gunning destroyed far more birds than anyone nowadays would wish, but society did wake up to its mistakes and stopped uncontrolled hunting. Even so, 20 years after the formal end of market hunting and 25 years or more after the start of legislated hunting controls, biologist Frederick C. Lincoln wrote in *The Waterfowl Flyways of North America*, a 1935 U.S. Department of Agriculture report: "There is today indisputable evidence that the waterfowl of North America have alarmingly decreased in numbers. There is also a growing conviction that special precautions must be taken to prevent the extermination of these valuable migratory species."

Populations continued to decline after that report until the 1980s, when North American waterfowl populations hit their lowest levels in history. It is obvious that, with or without guns, humans are the major reason that migratory birds no longer blacken the skies.

As market hunting declined, restaurants turned to domestically grown meats, and hunting in general became a minority sport, one would have thought the decoy would become an anachronism. Exactly the opposite happened. By the early 1920s most of the original decoy factories had closed, but here and there, individual carvers sitting quietly in shanty workshops continued to whittle decoys for enjoyment, personal use or use by other sportspeople. Out of those shanties the decoy, silent and shadowy, drifted into the spotlight of the American folk art scene.

Although the days of market hunting are long gone, waterfowl continue to have significant economic impact on North America. The U.S. Fish and Wildlife Service estimates that by 1985 approximately 3.2 million people were spending nearly $1 billion annually to hunt waterfowl. Interest in waterfowl and other migratory birds had grown in other areas as well. About 18.6 million people in 1985 observed, photographed and otherwise appreciated waterfowl and spent $2 billion for the pleasure of doing so.

Overleaf: Pair of Mallards (*c.* 1920)

Pair of Mallards
(*c.* 1920)

CHAPTER THREE
The Artful Decoy

Detail of Red-breasted
Merganser (year unknown)

The indigenous man who 2,100 years ago carefully wove reeds into the decoy shapes found at Lovelock Cave, Nevada, had much in common with the decoy carvers who evolved from the market hunting era. Each had the goal of making lures to entice ducks into killing range. Each found joy and satisfaction in using his individual talents to create the best piece possible. Hunting is a pursuit rich in rituals, many centered on the careful crafting and maintenance of hunting tools. Pride in one's equipment—its appearance as well as function—is part of the hunter's psyche.

Little creativity was expressed during the prime market gunning years, during which spreads of hundreds of decoys were used to draw migratory birds. Market hunters needed rugged decoys that were light and easily transportable. A reasonable facsimile—something that looked like a duck at a glance—was all that was required, and in the earlier days little attention was paid even to making distinctions between species. Supplying the

Hollow Redhead drake (*c.* 1935)

One of North America's most prolific decoy carvers was Cliff Avann (1891–1965). He is believed to have carved more than 10,000 decoys in his life and was called the "eight-minute decoy maker" after being challenged to show how fast he could carve a bird.

burgeoning market hunting industry required that production not be slowed by the performance of detailed work.

That changed, however, as America passed through dramatic industrial and cultural changes in the last half of the nineteenth century. By the end of the Civil War, America was no longer a frontier where the main daily work was survival. Fewer people needed to hunt regularly in order to eat, and individual hunting began its transformation into a recreational pursuit. Private hunt clubs opened as early as the 1850s, and with the growth of sport hunting came the pride in one's equipment that produced more realistic decoys. Sport hunters usually did not use the large layouts of the market hunters, so more time was spent on the detailed carving of fewer decoys. Sport hunters did kill birds by the hundreds, however, and sometimes sold extras to defray expenses or avoid wastage. There is the story of the legendary George Warrin, a one-armed club shooter and carver, who with two friends took 3,000 birds on Lake St. Clair in 1865.

The development of hunting clubs was as responsible as anything for the advancement of decoy carving to an artful pursuit. As passenger rail travel became more frequent and comfortable, wealthy professionals and businessmen rode the trains out of Washington, Boston, New York, Chicago and Detroit to hunt clubs and resorts established in the waterfowl areas. There, members shot over fine decoys from comfortable blinds, relaxing later with drinks and tobacco in the warm comfort of clubby surroundings and fraternal conversation. Hired help cleaned their catches, cooked their meals, carved their decoys and cared for their equipment.

In 1881, the Chicago, Rock Island and Pacific Railway advertised trips to Snachwine Lake, 120 miles (190 km) from Chicago, where excellent shooting, accommodations, decoys and boats were available. The St. Louis, Iron Mountain and Southern Railway offered special hunting cars, cooks and complete outfitting for waterfowlers wanting to shoot ducks in Arkansas.

Long Island was popular for shooters. Rich New Yorkers rode the trains to its many hunt clubs and resorts, where fine shooting pieces and excellence in decoy making were

"It is my wish that the decoy duck of American duck shooting have a pedigree of its own."
—Joel Barber

Drake and hen Whistlers (c. 1930)

much admired. Famous clubs existed throughout the continent: Carroll's Island Club on Chesapeake Bay, the Wapanocka Club in eastern Arkansas and the Long Pointe and St. Clair Flats clubs on Lake Erie, where marshes in both the U.S. and Canada attracted affluent hunters from Detroit, Toronto and New York.

Caretakers and guides at the clubs often carved, and the members supported their work, commissioning decoy sets to meet regional hunting conditions. That's how legendary Cape Cod carver Elmer Crowell got his start. Dr. John C. Phillips, a wealthy Boston physician, hired him in 1900 to manage his hunting camp at Wenham Lake, north of Boston. Crowell, a market gunner and cranberry farmer, carved working decoys as well as some non-functional pieces for the club members, and in 1912 he turned to full-time carving from East Harwich, Massachusetts. His work is considered some of the finest in the world and has drawn record prices at auction.

It was the demand from sport hunters that allowed carvers like Crowell to turn to carving as full-time work. Every community with a significant waterfowl population had its own carvers with their distinctive styles. Probably the most famous were the Ward Brothers of Maryland's Eastern Shore. Stephen and Lemuel Ward were born in 1895 and 1896 and became barbers in Crisfield, Maryland, Steve running his own shop at home while Lem worked for others. As they waited for customers, the brothers took to whittling ducks to pass the time, and soon they found that while a haircut brought in 15 cents, a decoy could fetch $1. They began working as a team to produce more volume.

Like other carvers, the Wards made a few ornamental decoys as early as the 1920s, but it wasn't until the late 1940s that their work became highly decorative and they began advertising themselves as Wildfowl Counterfeiters in Wood. In 1948 they entered the New York Decoy Show and won "Best in Show" and a number of other categories. Their fame grew, and presidents Franklin D. Roosevelt, Harry Truman and Lyndon Johnson were said to have hunted over the Wards' decoys. As other regional carvers noted their successes, they too began to make birds as collectibles. The Wards helped establish Maryland as the spiritual capital of wildfowl carving. The Ward Museum of Wildfowl Art and the Ward Foundation, in Salisbury, Maryland, were established in their

The popularity of decoy collecting grew significantly during the 1960s and 1970s in the wake of some significant exhibitions. The U.S. pavilion at Expo 67 in Montreal displayed an impressive collection of regional decoys. In 1970, a traveling exhibition of William Mackey decoys was displayed at the World's Fair in Osaka, Japan.

Rare Redhead hens (c. 1925)

There are likely more wooden duck decoys in museums, antique shops and individual homes than in the field. The number of people carving genuine hunting decoys for sale has dwindled to a mere handful across North America. One of the reasons is cost. If a carver takes eight hours to carve and paint a decoy and wants $10 an hour for his time, that decoy costs $80. Some of the few remaining carvers often charge $100 to $200 per working decoy. Hunting shops sell decoys made of man-made materials for a fraction of that cost.

honor. In 1974, Salisbury College awarded them honorary doctorates. The Ward Foundation's World Championship Carving Competition is the premiere competition of its kind in North America.

The dawn of the twentieth century was also the golden era for the factories, notably Detroit's J. N. Dodge and W. J. Mason, and Stevens Decoy Factory of Weedsport, New York. These companies turned out tens of thousands of decoys in the late nineteenth and early twentieth centuries. The George Petersen Decoy Company at 276–278 Division Street in Detroit is believed to have been the first large decoy factory, opening around 1880 before being taken over by Jasper Dodge in 1884. It was followed by Mason in 1896. Petersen advertised top-quality mallards for $9 a dozen in 1882.

Mason Factory decoys are the most famous, and the Mason story provides a good illustration of the business of the times. William Mason owned a sporting goods store, and his interest in waterfowl hunting prompted him to open a decoy factory at his home on Tuscola Street in Detroit. The factory expanded, with Mason hiring craftsmen known for producing high-quality cedar birds. Mason was sharp on detail, and he observed and sketched ducks in order to intensify the realism of his productions. He did not live to see the company hit its peak, dying in 1905 from a fever that struck him after lying in a marsh sketching birds. Herbert, one of his three sons, took over the business.

All Mason decoys were carved by hand until 1903, when the company installed duplicating lathes for making bodies; heads continued to be carved by hand. Skilled painters finished each decoy individually, creating the unusual situation where thousands of factory decoys were all slightly different. The care taken in their production extended to floating each one in a washtub to check for balance and weighting. They sold in shops for $4 to $12 a dozen, depending on grade and detail factors such as whether eyes were glass, tack or painted. Mason designs were simple, with little detail except in the bills. They were known for their high-quality painting and the distinct swirl pattern that became their trademark.

The Mason Factory closed in 1924, a victim of the times and of a move into the more profitable sideline of supplying auto finishes for Ford. Most other factories had already shut down in the wake of the legislated hunting controls. Many others opened and closed during the 1930s as the Depression sent hunters back to the marshes to feed themselves and their families.

Harlequin Duck
(c. 1930)

Meanwhile, individual carvers like Crowell survived and flourished as membership in affluent hunt camps became a status symbol. The independent craftsman offered something a factory could not: specialized carving for the locality. Hunting conditions vary wildly from one region to another. Chesapeake Bay and other coastal areas feature big water and tides. Big water means much bobbing, so large, more stable decoys are

Overleaf: Pair of drake Mergansers (c. 1930)

Previous page:
Pair of Blue Bills
(*c.* 1920)

Charles E. Wheeler
of Stratford,
Connecticut, who
won the grand
championship at the
first American decoy
show in 1923, is one
of the icons of decoy
carving. He was
most commonly
known as Shang, the
nickname that had
been given to him at
age 13. Wheeler was
tall and thin, and
the nickname came
from "Langshang,"
one of the tallest
breeds of chickens.

needed. These decoys would look out of place in the placid bayous of Louisiana or the tiny potholes of the plains. Some areas required rigs of dozens of decoys, and setting out heavy, solid blocks was laborious, so carvers sometimes created hollow, lighter decoys. Availability of materials also created regional differences. Cork decoys were used in Long Island at one time, and local lore is that the raw material came from cork-filled life jackets that drifted ashore after shipwrecks. Some decoys were carved with overhanging breasts that allowed them to ride better in slush ice. Others were shaped to create a rocking motion, the look of ducks moving on the water.

Each carver had a local following, and if his work was especially good, word spread and attracted regional and national attention. For instance, in the Midwest, Charles Perdew (1874–1963) was the most revered of the Illinois River Valley carvers, and his work gained national renown. Charles E. (Shang) Wheeler (1872–1949) of Stratford, Connecticut, was well known locally but attained wider fame by winning the grand championship of the first-ever decoy show in 1923. In Louisiana, Laurent Vincent gained a reputation by using brown glass from beer bottles for fashioning decoy eyes. Captain Ellis Parker of Beach Haven, New Jersey, managed the Middle Sedge Gun Club on Long Island and was known as one of the most prolific carvers. He is said to have carved between 30,000 and 40,000 decoys in the course his life.

In most cases these were uncomplicated men—farmers, barbers, shopkeepers. They carved in woodsheds and shanty workshops and in chairs placed around the general store stove. The more they carved, the more they refined their work, adding details such as feathers and teeth. Their creative urges dictated that they strive to carve figures as close as possible to the birds they saw on the water. That meant carving sleeping ducks, preening ducks, ducks calling and ducks drinking. It was argued, and still is, that detail does little to attract ducks at a distance. Decoration on a shotgun doesn't make it shoot more accurately, either. However, some refinements were practical. Feathering, for instance, creates edging to reduce the glare that causes approaching ducks to flare. Non-game birds were carved too, sometimes out of a simple desire to do something different, but often to place near working decoys to create a more natural scene. A carved heron placed in the shallows near a rig of decoys was a sign of serenity and security.

More elaborate carving inevitably led to calls for public display of the best work. The first known decoy showing was in 1876 at the International Centennial Exposition in

Hollow Black Duck
(year unknown)

Philadelphia. After that, decoys began to appear on mantels, but collecting did not become widespread until Joel Barber, a New York architect, popularized it early in the twentieth century. Barber studied the history of decoys, regarding them as works of art that illustrated an important part of American history. He joined with the Howell's Point Anti-Dusker Society in 1923 to hold the first decoy show in Bellport, Long Island. It was organized in part to support a campaign against the hunting of black ducks at dusk, a practice some hunters complained was reducing that bird's population. In 1934, Barber published *Wild Fowl Decoys*, still considered one of the best books ever written on this subject.

Overleaf: Drake and hen Whistlers (*c.* 1930)

Other shows in other cities followed the Bellport exhibition, including New York in 1924 and 1931, the year that the decoy truly entered the world of folk art. That year, the Newark Museum held an exhibition of folk art sculpture, and decoys were included. The decision to place decoys alongside ships' figureheads and cigar-store Indians established the decoy in the world of folk art and prompted other museums, as well as individuals, to begin collections. As collections grew, shows and competitions attracted more attention. The shows originally promoted hunting decoys, but interest over the years turned to showpiece carving and collection. The decoy as artwork reached a new level of respect in 1966 when author-collector William J. Mackey Jr. displayed two hundred pieces from his collection at the IBM Gallery of Arts and Sciences in New York City. A year later in Montreal, decoys were displayed prominently in the U.S. pavilion at Expo 67.

By the 1960s, decoys were being carved almost exclusively as decorative pieces. Hunters had turned to light, durable birds manufactured out of plastic, Styrofoam and other synthetics. Factory molding allowed mass production of decoys with every lifelike detail imaginable and a lifespan greater even than the hunter's. Technology has advanced factory decoys to the point where they can now move, flap their wings and quack. Battery-operated "motoducks" are now at the center of a controversy as hunters debate the ethics of using them. A California Waterfowl Association survey has found that almost 60 percent of its members

Joel D. Barber, the New York City architect and pioneer promoter of decoys as art, is said to have never hunted ducks. He did carve decoys, however, and was drawn to them not just for their artistic merit but due to the history of decoy hunting and the men who made them.

In 1999, Illinois State granted $100,000 for the restoration of the Perdew Home as part of the Charles Perdew Museum. Charles Perdew of Henry, Illinois, and his wife Edna, a painter, produced some of the most famous decoys in the Midwest.

Detail of Merganser drake (year unknown)

believe motorized decoys should be banned if it is proven they reduce waterfowl populations. Some members argue that motorized decoys remove the need for many hunting skills and are doubling and tripling duck kills.

Interest in the art of decoys and in their collection created an explosion of written material starting in the 1960s. The middle of that decade saw the publication of two important works: *The Art of the Decoy* by dealer-historian Adele Earnest and Mackey's *American Bird Decoys*. The magazine *Decoy Collector's Guide* began publishing in 1963. In the decades since, hundreds of books, magazines, papers and reports have expanded interest in collecting and in decorative carving as a hobby. The fascination with decoys has also spread into the world of antiques, where rare decoys now fetch remarkable prices.

Green-winged Teal (year unknown)

Overleaf: Red-breasted Mergansers (year unknown)

CHAPTER FOUR

The Decoy as Art and Collectible

Detail of Pintail drake
(*c*. 1940)

Decoys appear to swim against the current in the art world. One of the reasons for collecting art is that each piece is unique. Collectors want little to do with multiples, objects made common by mass production. There is no question that decoys were mass-produced, not just by factories but by full-time carvers like the Wards. Many are rough and simple carvings whittled by hunters with no training in the arts. How is it, then, that a factory decoy can fetch hundreds of thousands of dollars at auction?

Obviously, some decoys are valuable because they are rare. Crowell's sleeping Canada goose is one of a kind. Other carvers did commissioned or special carvings while turning out dozens of routine blocks for the marshes. Rarity aside, there is another important aspect to consider. Decoys, especially older, cruder blocks, cannot be viewed solely from the perspective of someone schooled in art. An essential part of decoy art is the culture

Drake Wood Duck (*c*. 1950)

Collecting decoys has become a global activity which constantly attracts new participants. People take to decoy collecting for many reasons. Decoys are pieces of art and add to the decor of homes. Some people collect them as an investment because their value has increased remarkably over the years. Probably the most important reason for collecting, however, is that decoys are symbols of North America's incredible waterfowl history, a history that closely followed the development of North America. Decoys also have become symbols of conservation — beautiful reminders of how we must do more to protect the world's environment.

it represents, a folksy culture in which whittling was done in social settings, amidst conversation and as a way of passing the time.

North American folk art flourished in the eighteenth and nineteenth centuries, with common folk producing weather vanes, shop signs, quilts, figureheads for ships, primitive paintings and a variety of crafts. While folk art flourished, it held no real interest for the people with the wealth to support it. That changed in 1930 when the Newark Museum staged American Primitives, an exhibition of 83 folk paintings. That event seemed to be the spark that ignited genuine interest in gathering folk collections, and the 30 years following the Great Depression saw steady growth in the recognition of folk art.

Interest in decoys paralleled the growth of American folk art during the mid-twentieth century. Those were the years when decoy carving evolved from utilitarian to decorative, combining aspects of artifact and sculpture. Since the 1960s decoys have developed a more diverse appeal. They remain of special interest to hunters, who view them as totems recalling the golden days of hunting. Others now see them as serious art, worthy of large expenditures. Still others want them for home decorating and as symbols of cultures and times past. This growing interest has inflated prices, which began to move up dramatically in the early 1970s.

The Influence of the McCleery Collection

The death of William Mackey in the early 1970s marked the beginning of a new era in collecting. His vast array of decoys came to auction in the summer of 1973, and Dr. James Merida McCleery of Pasadena, Texas, began what he envisioned as an unprecedented masterworks decoy collection. McCleery, a Houston pathologist whose ability to walk was lost to polio, bought a William Bowman curlew that had been a key part of the Mackey collection. When the bidding ended, he paid $10,500 for the bird, astounding the decoy world and establishing him as the leader in North American decoy collecting.

McCleery held his position at the top until his death in 1999, and his influence changed decoy collecting forever. No one before him had put together a collection so

Lowhead Blue Bill (c. 1900)

Male and female
Buffleheads (*c.* 1960)

broad, including pieces from diverse regions ranging from Canada to Louisiana, Chesapeake to Oregon. At the Sotheby and Guyette/Schmidt auction on January 22, 2000, McCleery's collection again astonished the decoy world: the sleeping Canada goose by Elmer Crowell went for $684,500, a Mason Factory drake wood for $384,500. More than 1,100 bidders participated, with 700 pieces selling for a total of more than $8 million. Sales of calls, shotgun shell boxes and other related items pushed the auction total above $11 million.

The rise in prices over the past 30 years is illustrated by a Mason Factory curlew that sold at the 1973 Mackey auction for $1,600; the same piece brought $21,275 at the January 2000 McCleery auction. One Crowell decoy sold for $900 at an auction in 1968. Another went for $300,000 in the early eighties, and the first auction of this century has seen Crowell work pushing $700,000.

The downside of all this attention is that collecting is not as easy, or uncomplicated, as it used to be. At shows and auctions, stories abound of the good old days when a person could fill a car trunk with decoys during a Saturday afternoon drive in the country. Baskets of decoys sold cheap or were given away by people who saw them as old working tools that had outlived their usefulness and were therefore of little value. These days, most decoys are obtained through catalogues, at auctions or through enterprises that intend to make money from the transaction. Prices, even for lesser blocks, are significant, and there is a danger of paying for frauds or pieces whose value is not close to the asking price. It is still possible to build an interesting collection on smaller amounts of money if you take time to decide what you want from a collection and spend time learning and planning how to go about it.

Resources for studying, discussing, researching and collecting are numerous and expanding. Carving and collecting clubs can be found in almost every region of the U.S. and Canada as well as in other countries. Shows and competitions are numerous throughout the northern two-thirds of the continent. As with every other hobby or pastime, the

One of the world's outstanding decoy collections will be given away as a donation. Harvey Pitt of Du Quoin, Illinois, whose 1,800-piece collection includes blocks dating to the 1870s, announced in 2001 that he is giving it all to McKendree College, where he earned a biology degree in 1950. The college will sell the collection after Pitt's death and use the money to establish a scholarship fund for biology students. Part of Pitt's collection, including 100 Mason blocks and 19 Ward brothers originals, is kept at his home and attracts 2,000 visitors a year.

Rare pair of hollow Lowhead Whistlers (c. 1900)

"Decoys are distinctive among folk arts because they are strictly a North American phenomenon. All the others [folk arts] can trace their roots overseas, but decoys were created on this continent as a response to the incredible natural world the settlers found here. For most of us, decoys are a link to a different order and to a different time."
— Bob Shaw, curator of Vermont's Shelbourne Museum, as quoted in Traditions in Wood (Camden House, 1987)

Internet is a valuable research tool and provides excellent communications between carvers, collectors and other interested persons.

Probably the most important part of collecting is deciding what you want. The best rule in collecting anything for pleasure is to get what you like. This maxim has been illustrated time and again in many areas of art. Thirty years ago a couple on a limited budget bought a print of an attractive young woman protectively holding a baby in her arms. It cost $14, including framing, at the local five-and-dime. Its value probably isn't much more today, but everyone who has visited the couple's house over three decades has commented on what a striking image it is.

Collecting decoys from close to home, or from areas you are intimately acquainted with, can also increase the pleasure. Knowing an area's history and the stories of some of its families often makes detailed research easier and allows you to talk about your decoys with more confidence.

Auctions are excellent and exciting places to learn about decoy collecting. Larger auctions, offering hundreds of blocks for sale, provide an opportunity to view many different kinds of decoys and to shmooze with as many types of collectors. Smaller auctions are more frequent and intimate, allowing chances to ask questions that might seem silly at a larger event but are necessary to building knowledge. Swap markets are set up in parking

Bufflehead (c. 1950)

Overleaf: Hollow Canvasback drake (c. 1960)

Previous page:
Pintail drake (c. 1940)

lots or motel rooms near to an auction site, and browsing and chatting at these places can uncover valuable information. Auctions involving decoys can be found in most regions of North America several times a year, and at least once a month in popular decoy areas such as the Midwest.

A catalogue of the pieces offered at an auction might be available, free or for a price. It might be simply a sheet with a list or, in the case of a larger operation, a high-quality publication detailing each piece and giving conditions of sale, estimates of the going prices and payment terms. Catalogues from past auctions can be ordered, at roughly $15 to $40 each, and are a prime source of information about decoys. Catalogues from the McCleery auction in January 2000 were selling for $47 later in the year and were in limited supply. Decoy catalogues have also begun to appear online.

Canada remains a place to get decoys at lower cost. Decoys were carved and used extensively in the Maritimes, Quebec, along the Great Lakes and throughout the Canadian Prairies, but the Canadian collecting market is not as hot as in the U.S. Interesting decoys can still be bought for $100 CAD, and the most expensive have yet to go beyond the $20,000 to $30,000 CAD range. The McCleery collection included Canadian decoys by John Wells of Toronto (1861–1953), who carved for royalty. His most sought-after decoys go for up to $10,000 CAD. However, experts predict that Canadian decoy prices will rise. There were indications of this in 2000 when a pair of green-winged teal by Ken Anger of Dunville, Ontario, sold for US$11,275, which was well above the estimate.

Many older Canadian hunters are giving up the sport because new gun laws require them to spend upwards of $500 CAD for firearms possession and acquisition licences. They also will have to pay to register each firearm by the year 2003. During the early stages of implementing these laws there were signs that hunters were selling off their equipment. Also, collectors from the U.S. have the distinct advantage of a currency rate that at the time of this writing makes the U.S. dollar worth roughly 50 percent more than the Canadian.

Bufflehead hen (c. 1950)

The Fraudulent Decoy

Where there is money, there is fraud. That simple tenet of commercial crime investigation applies to every commodity ever sold, including decoys. Just as taxation increases opportunities for smugglers, soaring decoy prices offer money-making chances to counterfeiters and con artists. A shop full of tools and a silver tongue are a good beginning for anyone wanting to get started in the fake folk art trade. Add to that collector gullibility and you have an excellent setting for fraud.

Fakery in early furniture, glass and hundreds of other collectibles has been constant since folk art started attracting attention and significant prices. Imitations are everywhere. Furniture is "antiqued" to create a wear effect and sold in stores. Radios are produced to look like the old classics of the forties. Even replicas of old automobiles are being produced. In most cases, however, these items are sold as imitations, with no attempt to fool anyone.

Copying of art pieces is common. Copyists produce exact likenesses of works for their own pleasure, to gain experience and to make money. Genuine copyists usually sign their work and make no attempt to misrepresent it. In the decoy world some copyists don't identify their work, and without this ethic the buyer is easily fooled. Early waterfowl decoy carvers seldom signed their works, although factories often stamped their decoys with a name or symbol. Experts say that many of the Ward Brothers decoys currently in existence were in fact never

Whistling was a popular way to attract shorebirds during early hunting days. Some hunters learned to imitate the whistling sounds of these birds but many carved or bought whistles that could produce sounds like those made by popular shorebirds. Shorebird whistles have become valued collectibles.

Canvasback drake (*c.* 1920)

94

touched by Lem or Steve Ward. The 1980s saw replication of Michigan fish decoys from the 1930s. So much copying has been done that even experts have difficulty telling the real from the fake.

Decoy fraud ranges from producing outright fakes to concealing a decoy's identity in order to raise its price. Tumble washing, staining and other forms of artificial aging are used to make newer decoys look antique. Even honest decoys are not always completely original, but the changes should be obvious to the buyer, and ideally will be documented. A decoy in its original state carries more value, and any attempt to preserve or enhance its appearance without informing the buyer is fraudulent. Repairs and repainting are sometimes undertaken to improve the condition, and therefore the value, of older decoys. Some old decoys may have been retouched when they were being used or have undergone extensive repair over the years. There is nothing wrong with buying a decoy that has been legitimately retouched. Much rests on how the repainting was done— whether it followed the original patterns and presents an accurate picture of the original. Repairs do pull value down, depending on their extent and how they were effected.

Where you buy can increase the chance of getting stuck with a fake or paying an inflated price for something that has been altered. Auctions and shows present birds from qualified dealers and collectors who know the business and have reputations to protect. Few experienced dealers are found at street fairs or flea markets, and people offering decoys in those circumstances are frequently not knowledgeable.

Buying decoys should always involve caution, questioning and research. Taking your time, asking for a lot of details, and taking photos is important. Examining many decoys builds a memory bank of things to look out for: a loose neck joint, which indicates that a head has been removed; oxidized paint, which appears older than it is; a decoy which is heavier than it should be or that smells of fresh cedar despite its supposed age; a bird that simply looks too good.

A network of knowledgeable friends and associates is a wonderful backstop when collecting decoys. They offer different views and ask questions you haven't thought of, and

Museum collections dedicated to the history of waterfowling exist throughout most parts of the United States and Canada. Probably the most famous is the Havre de Grace Decoy Museum, located on the Susquehanna Flats at Havre de Grace, Maryland. The museum contains 1,200 decoys and decorative carvings, many by waterfowl masters such as the Ward brothers.

Bufflehead drake (c. 1976)

their experience becomes part of your own. In the end the buyer still has to make up his or her own mind, but good decisions come from a strong knowledge base built through observation, research and talking to experienced people.

William J. Mackey devised a chart system for evaluating decoys, allowing points for the carver or manufacturer, the rarity of the decoy and its condition. He also had a column in which points were subtracted for negatives, such as painted eyes or never having been repainted. Points were added for being oversize and for an absence of blemishes. He suggested that a collector should consider the following items when evaluating a decoy:

- its historical associations
- unusual positions, such as preening or feeding
- unusual features of construction
- unusual construction materials, for example whalebone bills for shorebirds or surface coatings such as burlap or skin
- paint techniques such as shading or special textures

Decoy evaluation is a complicated process, but Mackey's system offers a starting point.

Studying Ducks and Decoys

Learning about waterfowl enhances the joy of collecting and is mandatory for anyone thinking of carving. It is important to be able to identify ducks and to possess a basic knowledge of their anatomy and behavior.

Ducks can be divided into two groups: divers and dabblers. Divers are bottom-feeders, found mainly on larger bodies of water. Dabblers are surface-feeders that frequent rivers, ponds and small lakes. The wings of dabblers are larger in proportion to their bodies than those of divers and allow them to land and take off like helicopters. Divers take off like 747s, running across the water to gain the speed to get airborne. Divers' feet are large and set farther back in the body than those of dabblers.

"I have always considered decoys as a tool....That some are more attractive than others, ride better, are more durable and qualify as works of art, cannot be denied, but I view any decoy first with the eye of the hunter."
— William J. Mackey, Jr., author of *American Bird Decoys*

Overleaf: Pair of Mallards (year unknown)

Eider hen (c. 1950)

Previous page: Male
and female Hooded
Mergansers (c. 1940)

Ducks display a lot of attitude. They can be social, tuk-tuking cheekily to their neighbors. They can be sleepy, with head folded into a wing. They can be very excitable. A tilted bill suggests a duck swallowing a morsel plucked from the water. Carvers who were able to capture some attitude produced decoys that not only were aesthetically pleasing but often lured better in competitive hunting areas. A mix of birds preening, feeding and calling always made for a confident decoy rig that would pull real ducks from the skies.

Some knowledge of materials is also helpful to the collector. Decoys have been made from papier mâché, synthetics, cork, twigs, cloth, metal and any number of woods. Wood was always the standard because it withstands the punishment of being tossed in and out of boats and battered by ice. Hardwoods were not used because they do not float well. Basswood was considered ideal—it is fine-grained and easy to carve—but pine and cedar were more popular because they were easier to get. Cedar offered the distinct advantage of resisting rot brought on by wetness. Tupelo was widely used in some of the southern U.S. states.

Balsa wood became popular for decoys after the Second World War, when surplus military life rafts made of balsa were dumped on the market. The Ward Brothers produced bodies of balsa for a time, but the balsa trend died because it was based on artificially low prices. Balsa is porous and difficult to carve. When the sealing on a balsa decoy fails, it will draw water and become heavy.

Insights into the process of carving are easily obtained by attending one of the many meetings, lectures and workshops on carving held throughout the continent. Carvers are happy to pass along tips and experiences. Larry Barth, award-winning wildfowl carver from Stahlstown, Pennsylvania, offered the following insights to a meeting of carvers in the summer of 2000. The insights apply more to modern bird carvings than to old hunting decoys, but they give a glimpse of what is in the carver's mind.

Do-it-yourself decoy kits were once popular throughout North American waterfowl hunting areas. The kits allowed amateur decoy makers to pour foam pellets into an aluminum mold and melt them in home ovens. These foam decoys had to be painted and weighted down, and were also somewhat delicate, but they were popular because of their light weight.

- It is important to work in natural light. Soft lines are essential, because hard edges cannot be painted over.
- Crisp, clean detail is vital, and carvers should strive for total integrity under the paint.

- When doing the feathers, the carver is really painting the bird. Paint will not hide poor carving.
- No carved bird should be made perfect. Perfect reads as fake. Take enough perfection out to make it real.

Black Duck and
Green-winged Teal
(c. 1945)

Duck Stamps and Duck Calls

Decoy carvers of old would be shocked to learn of the prices now placed on their hand-worked blocks. Even more shocked would be the inventors of the U.S. Migratory Bird Hunting Stamp Act of 1934, a legislative initiative aimed at starting modest acquisition and restoration of wetlands. It grew into an amazingly successful government program that is now credited with preserving five million acres (two million ha) of wetland in the National Wildlife Refuge System. The 1934 act was followed in 1937 by a federal tax on firearms and ammunition, which has also raised millions of dollars for wildlife conservation.

The duck stamp, as it was later called, was mandatory for all migratory bird hunters 16 years of age and older. The first one sold for $1, a high price during the Depression years but one that was nevertheless paid by 635,000 hunters. The price has increased over the years to $15 in 2000, and under the 1986 Emergency Wetlands Resources Act it will continue to increase over the next 10 years to raise even more funds for refuges. The sale of duck stamps has generated more than a quarter of a billion dollars for conservation.

Somewhere along the way, the stamps and the artwork from which they are produced became collectibles for hunters, investors, and stamp and art collectors. Anyone who purchased a stamp each year from 1934 to 2000 would have spent roughly $365. A mint set of all stamps is worth upwards of $10,000, depending on their condition.

The value of duck stamps as collectibles is enhanced by the fact that, compared with postage stamps, few are printed. Only about two million of the fiftieth-anniversary duck stamp were sold, compared with 123 million of the U.S. Postal Service's 20-cent stamp commemorating the same anniversary. Also, all unsold duck stamps are destroyed three years after issue, preserving the value of collected stamps. Mistakes in printing have been few, but there have been some errors that have made for higher value. There are a few 1991 king eider stamps missing the black engraving on the birds' breasts; these are worth $12,500 each.

Artwork for the duck stamps is chosen from among the entries in a national competition. Prices for the original artwork have been increasing steadily and now run as high as $50,000. Prints run anywhere from $250 to $10,000 or more.

There are an estimated 350,000 collectors of U.S. Federal duck stamps in North America. Many collect for philatelic reasons while others save them for their beauty. Some people save them simply because they know the money collected is used for waterfowl conservation projects.

The world championship of duck calling is held each November in Stuttgart, Arkansas. Contestants — all winners of sanctioned state and regional competitions — come from across the U.S. and Canada. The championship contest has been held in Stuttgart since 1936 and is part of the Wings Over the Prairie festival that celebrates waterfowl with a collectibles show, exhibits and seminars. The events attract more than 50,000 visitors each year.

Duck calling has evolved into a distinct sport. There is magic in making the right sounds and watching flying birds pick them up. They bob and weave, trying to analyze the situation before accepting the scene below and setting their wings against the wind to splash to a landing among the decoys. Early hunters learned mouth calling from the Native peoples. The human voice is limited in volume and tone, however, and not everyone has the knack. Hunters turned to devising instruments that could make duck sounds. The first handmade calls consisted of a metal strip sandwiched between two strips of curved wood. They were used in the mid-nineteenth century and were known as tongue pinchers because the metal strip would often cut the tongue.

Detail of drake and hen Whistlers (c. 1930)

The duck call evolved along the Mississippi flyway, notably in Illinois, where many of the legendary call makers lived and hunted. There the mallards and other dabbling ducks were plentiful and responded well to calling. On the eastern shore, however, diving ducks such as redheads and canvasbacks were not as responsive to calling.

Duck calls can still be had in the $100 range, but they can also run into the thousands and even above $10,000 for a rare carved call by Charlie Perdew. His basic calls were banded cedar, checkered walnut and painted mahogany. His carved calls generally sell in the $3,000 to $4,000 range, but the banded cedar go for $400 to $600.

Racks for storing calls are collected too, and they command prices into the thousands of dollars.

Overleaf: Hollow Canada Goose (c. 1948)

CHAPTER FIVE

Protecting Our Waterfowl Legacy

Detail of cross-hatched drake Whistler

Swamps, wetlands and overflow lands were a nuisance during the settlement of North America. They were dark and dangerous, largely impassable, incapable of producing worthwhile food, places of disease and decay. Settlers saw them as a blight to be drained, covered and made wholesome.

As market hunting entered its most intense period, the U.S. Congress took action to reclaim these so-called useless lands. It passed the first of the Swamp Lands Acts in 1849, unaware of the profound adverse effects the law would have on migratory birds many decades after the market guns were silenced. These acts turned swamplands over to the states for reclamation. They officially sanctioned the idea that wetlands are better drained and filled for settlement, an attitude that would dominate for more than a century. By the time things

Detail of male Wood Duck (c. 1972)

began to change, late in the twentieth century, more than half of North America's wetlands had disappeared and the migratory birds that used them were only fractions of previous populations.

The U.S. Fish and Wildlife Service (USFWS) estimates that between the 1780s and the 1980s the 48 contiguous states lost 54 percent of their 221 million acres (89 million hectares) of wetlands; that's 60 acres (24 hectares) an hour for two hundred years. California retains only 9 percent of its historic wetlands, Ohio 10 percent, Iowa 11 percent, Indiana and Missouri 13 percent. More than one-half of Connecticut's wetlands are gone as are half of the Florida Everglades and much of the marshland of the Chesapeake.

In Canada, the main nesting ground for North American waterfowl, wetland losses range from 29 to 71 percent since settlement. Studies on the Canadian Prairies show that an average of 59 percent of pothole basins and up to 79 percent of wetland plants are affected by farming each year. Human encroachment will continue to be a major threat. Demographers predict the population of the U.S. will increase by the equivalent of 15 New Yorks in the next 50 years, and Canada and Mexico will grow proportionately.

The Chesapeake Bay watershed, which encompasses one of the great wetland areas of North America, best illustrates the losses. This is one of the most productive ecosystems in the world, supporting 2,700 species of wildlife. However, siltation and pollution have deteriorated water quality and killed off aquatic vegetation important to wildlife survival. Blue crab populations, for example, are now at about 10 percent of their historic levels. In the area surrounding the Chesapeake, USFWS estimates that Maryland has lost 73 percent of its original wetlands, Virginia 42 percent and Pennsylvania 56 percent. Declining water quality affects humans as well as wildlife, especially those who rely on natural resources for their living.

Ducks Unlimited, prompted by the problems in the Chesapeake, has undertaken an ambitious restoration program there. By 2005, the organization plans to restore 25,000 acres (10,000 ha) of habitat and 2,400 miles (1,450 km) of streamside buffers. The goal is improved water quality and habitat, and the price tag $18 million.

The migration routes of waterfowl in North America are almost exclusively north-south, probably because of the continent's topographical features. Major mountain ranges, coasts and the largest river valleys all are north to south. Oddly, no two species follow the exact same route from beginning to end.

Detail of Green-winged Teal (year unknown)

Government agencies estimated that the autumn 2000 migration of North American ducks reached 90 million. That's a decline of 13 per cent from the 105 million of 1999 but is significantly better than the 1990 migration of 57 million which followed a decade of drought on the northern plains.

Loss of waterfowl and waterfowl habitat reached the alarm stage in the 1980s and frightened governments into action. The U.S. Congress passed the Emergency Wetland Resources Act in 1986 as an attempt to curtail wetland losses. Also in 1986, the U.S. and Canada agreed to a North American Waterfowl Management Plan aimed at restoring waterfowl populations by protecting and improving their habitat. Mexico joined the plan in 1994. It sets goals for 32 populations of ducks and calls for a breeding duck index of 62 million, which would produce an annual fall flight of 100 million ducks. Private and public conservation organizations have committed $1.6 billion to support the plan's goals to 2010.

Detail of Cork body Canvasback (c. 1920)

These initiatives have helped to slow the rate of migratory bird habitat loss. A USFWS study shows a net annual loss of 117,000 acres (47,000 ha) of wetland between 1985 and 1995, an improvement over the annual loss of 458,000 acres (185,000 ha) between 1950 and 1970, and 290,000 acres (117,000 ha) a year in the 1970s and 1980s. Although there is no precise figure for all the wetland acres that have been restored, the USFWS estimates that between 1987 and 1990 about 90,000 acres (36,400 ha) were added to the nation's wetland inventory.

Waterfowl appear to be benefiting. USFWS reported that 105 million ducks flew south in the autumn of 1999. That is a substantial increase over the modern-day record of 92 million in 1997. However, the fall flight for 2000 was predicted to be down again—to 90 million ducks, a 13 percent drop from 1999. Included in that figure were 11.3 million mallards, compared with 13.6 million in 1999. Goose numbers too were down, but biologists say that most populations remain healthy.

Today's conservation efforts are rooted in the concerns that arose during and immediately following the years of market hunting. The role of individuals in developing waterfowl conservation movements has been remarkable. George Grinnell, editor of *Forest and Stream* in the 1880s, helped to create the Audubon movement. Teddy Roosevelt took the advice of a lot of friends and promoted conservation laws. Individuals formed the American Bird Banding Association in 1909 and collected invaluable information on migratory bird patterns. Eleven years later banding had become so widespread that it was turned over to the U.S. Bureau of Biological Survey and the Canadian Wildlife Service, which were better organized and staffed to handle the work.

It was also an individual, not an organized research body, who did much to develop aerial counts of waterfowl. Frank C. Bellrose, binoculars in hand, traveled the Illinois River Valley in the late 1930s and 1940s by car and boat to record waterfowl numbers. In 1946 he experimented with

Overleaf: Pair of Shovelers (*c.* 1950)

aerial observations and noted that the waterfowl of the entire Illinois Valley could be thereby inventoried in one day rather than the one week required on the ground.

The impact of the individual in conservation work cannot be demonstrated more vividly than by the story of Jack Miner, who, with only three months' formal schooling, became North America's most famous early waterfowl conservationist. Miner was born in Ohio at the end of the Civil War and moved to Kingsville, Ontario, on the north shore of Lake Erie when he was 13. He became a market hunter and trapper, and turned to religion and conservation after the deaths of a brother, a daughter and his eldest son. In 1904, the year of his son's death, Miner flooded one of the family brickyard pits and stocked it with seven pinioned geese bought from a trapper. Soon he was attracting and feeding migratory birds.

Miner started bird banding in August 1909, and his first banded duck was recovered in South Carolina five months later. He continued to band thousands of birds, and the information recovered was used in the preparation of the North American Migratory Bird Treaty. A man who learned to read so he could study the Bible, Miner wrote two books, lectured and in 1936 gave an around-the-world radio address that prompted letters from 65 countries. He was awarded the Outdoor Life Gold Medal in 1929 for the "greatest achievement in wildlife conservation on the continent" and in 1943 the Order of the British Empire for "the greatest achievement in conservation in the British Empire."

Each year in early April, Canada observes National Wildlife Week in Miner's honor, and the Jack Miner Migratory Bird Foundation was established in

"Jack Miner's companionship with the birds and his service to them have made his work known and has warmed the hearts of good people everywhere. He has taught us all that there is always something to do for one who looks for something to do."
— auto pioneer Henry Ford

Foreground: Cross-hatched Hooded Merganser; background: cross-hatched drake Whistler

the 1930s in both Canada and the U.S. as a charitable institution. By the time of his death in 1944, Miner is said to have personally banded 50,000 ducks and 40,000 geese. His bird sanctuary at Kingsville continues the banding program to this day, and Bible verses such as "Fear God and Give Him Glory—Revelation 14:7" and "Be Not Afraid; Only Believe—Mark 5:36" are still printed on the sanctuary's bird bands. They are recovered throughout the continent every year and are collectibles.

Individuals' concern for vanishing waterfowl led to the creation in 1937 of Ducks Unlimited (DU), probably the world's most influential waterfowl conservation group. Dwight W. Huntington, editor of *Amateur Sportsman* magazine, founded the Game Conservation Society in 1912. That group evolved into the More Game Birds in America Foundation, which established DU and then turned all its assets over to it. DU now boasts 733,000 members, and in fiscal 2000 it raised $131 million for restoring and preserving waterfowl habitat. Its annual report to members said that DU efforts conserved 9.4 million acres (3.8 million ha) of waterfowl habitat in 2000. Much of the organization's funds are raised through events, such as dinners, organized by approximately 50,000 individuals who volunteer their time.

Governments and private conservation groups believe that the huge sums now being spent on wetland conservation are a good financial investment as well as a wise environmental one. There are hundreds of national and regional studies estimating the economic value of migratory birds. It's easy to put forward some impressive figures from any of these, but numbers can be made to support any argument. The essential point is that millions of North Americans spend billions of dollars each year hunting, watching, photographing and feeding waterfowl. A 1994 government survey showed that in Canada alone, 6.6 million citizens put out special feed for wildlife. That is more than 20 percent of the population.

The value of the interest in waterfowl is easily seen by visiting some of the museums and other historic sites throughout New England, or Point Pelee National Park in southern Ontario, where birdwatchers spend nearly $6 million a year on accommodation, food, travel and equipment to see such wonders as 40 different species of colorful migrating warblers.

Migratory birds do not recognize geopolitical boundaries, and because they don't, governments seem to exercise remarkable co-operation in trying to manage their popu-

The use of steel hunting shot has become critically important in North American waterfowl conservation. The United States banned lead shot in 1991, and Canada did so in 1999, because ducks, geese and other water birds ingest it when feeding from the bottoms of lakes, rivers and ponds in heavily hunted areas. A study by the Illinois Department of Natural Resources estimates that the reduction in lead poisoning prevented the loss of 1.4 million ducks in 1997 alone.

lations. Few issues draw the federal governments of the U.S., Canada and Mexico, plus their various provincial and state governments, so close together in a spirit of working for the common good. The three countries observe International Migratory Bird Day each spring to celebrate migratory birds and their importance in the natural word. Part of the day's purpose is to encourage people to help create a friendly environment for all birds.

It has become clear that the future of waterfowl is in the hands of humans: hunters, environmentalists, associations and governments. Hunting continues to take its toll, but it is monitored and regulated. Lead shot, which poisons waterfowl habitats, has been banned in many regions, and good hunting ethics are being promoted throughout the continent. More hunter education is needed to improve identification of the species and sex of ducks being shot at, and to lower the numbers of birds crippled each year in the field.

The most important work in waterfowl conservation is our management of the land, and this requires huge amounts of co-operation, smart thinking and money. Waterfowl need clean and abundant water to survive and reproduce. So do humans, but clean and plentiful water can no longer be taken for granted. Every year in the U.S. and Canada there are more reports of disease from bad water and communities issuing "boil water" directives because of infected water systems.

"What we do for migratory birds, even in our cities, has the potential to doom a species or to save it from extinction," USFWS director Jamie Rappaport Clark has said. "As communities keep growing and expanding, it is important to the health of their environment that they preserve vital open spaces close to home. It's good for the birds, good for the environment, and good for the people."

The U.S. Environmental Protection Agency says runoff from agricultural lands and urban areas is the primary source of pollutants in fresh water.

Overleaf: Hen and drake Wood Ducks (c. 1972)

Resources

Books

Barber, Joel. *Wild Fowl Decoys*. New York: Dover Publications, 1954.

The Bird Decoy: An American Art Form. Lincoln: University of Nebraska Press, 1976.

Bridenhagen, Keith, and Patrick Spielman. *Realistic Decoys*. New York: Sterling Publishing Co., 1984.

Earnest, Adele. *Art of the Decoy: American Bird Carvings*. Exton, Pennsylvania: Schiffler Publishing Co., 1981.

Kangas, Linda and Gene. *The Collector's Guide to Decoys*. Radnor, Pennsylvania: Wallace-Homestead Book Co., 1992.

Mackey Jr., William J. *American Bird Decoys*. New York: E. P. Dutton and Co., 1965.

Starr, George Ross. *How to Make Working Decoys*. New York: Winchester Press, 1978.

Walsh, Harry M. *Outlaw Gunner*. Cambridge, Maryland: Tidewater Publications, 1971.

Whistling Wings, Whittled Ducks and Wetlands. Milwaukee Public Museum, 1996.

Web Sites

Ward Brothers Museum: *www.wardmuseum.org*

Ducks Unlimited: *www.ducks.org*

FishDecoy.com: *www.fishdecoy.com*

U.S. Fish and Wildlife Service (migratory birds): *birds.fws.gov*

Canadian Wildlife Service: *www.cws-scf.ec.gc.ca/cwshom_e*

Decoy magazine: *www.decoymag.com*

Waterfowler magazine: *www.waterfowler.com/frames/index1*

Waterfowl links: *home.att.net/~DanCowell/page2*

How to weave a Native duck decoy: *www.nativetech.org/decoy/DecoyInstr*